INSTITUTES OF THE SISTERS

OF

SAN SISTO OF ROME

and

STATUTES OF THE SISTERS

OF

SAINT MARY MAGDALENE

Institutes of the Sisters of San Sisto of Rome *and* Statutes of the Sisters of Saint Mary Magdalene, *edited by* Andre Simon, Fribourg, Switzerland, 1918; *translated by* Sister Mary Martin Jacobs, O.P.

DNS PUBLICATIONS

Dominican Nuns of Summit
543 Springfield Avenue
Summit, New Jersey 07901
summitdominicans.org/dns-publications

TABLE OF CONTENTS

TRANSLATOR'S PREFACE

When Mother Marie Rosaria, O.P. translated the *Rule of San Sisto* in 1969, the Golden Jubilee year of the Monastery of Our Lady of the Rosary, Summit, she envisioned it as a "service in renewal and adaptation." She used the only edition available to her, the French translation made by J.J. Berthier, O.P. from the text in the Vatican archives, and printed in his translation of the *Chronicles of San Sisto.* She never dreamed that this, the only translation into English of the primitive legislation of the nuns of the Order, would still be in demand thirty-five years later and would have attained over the years a world-wide audience.

Unfortunately, a translation of a translation is never as accurate as a translation from the original, and Berthier did his work in French before Andre Simon published his critical edition of the Latin text in 1918. Simon's edition became standard and is the one that Vicaire commented on in an appendix to his *St. Dominic and His Times.*[1] However I was not able to obtain a copy of Simon's edition until 2003, when one of the friars at the Dominican House of Studies, Washington DC made me several copies from their library.

Almost immediately, I began a fresh translation from Simon's edition, which includes not only the *Rule of San Sisto*, but also the *Statutes of the Penitents of Saint Mary Magdalene.* These latter, as Simon,[2] Vicaire,[3] and R. Creytens[4] point out, were copied, in most places verbatim, from the constitutions of the Friars of the

---

[1] M-H Vicaire, O.P., *St. Dominic and His Times,* tr. Kathleen Pond, Alt Publishing company, Green Bay, WI, 1964; Appendix VIII, p. 428
[2] See below, p. 33
[3] Vicaire, op. cit., p. 428
[4] R. Creytens, O.P., "Les constitutions primitives des soeurs dominicaines de Montargis," *Archivum Fratrum Praedicatorum* XVII (1947), 41-84

Order of Preachers, as these are found in the Rodez manuscript which dates to 1228. They were then adapted for nuns. Vicaire asserts, on the basis of internal evidence, that the adaptation was originally done for an individual monastery of Dominican nuns, then applied to the Penitents of St. Mary Magdalene.[5] This is an attractive hypothesis, but impossible to prove conclusively. Creytens is of the opinion that, whether or not the *Statutes* were ever used by a Dominican monastery, such monasteries were, of necessity, making similar adaptations.[6] In any case, the *Statutes* as they stand apply to the Penitents and to them only. They are of interest mainly because they fill up a lacuna in our progressive collection of legislation adapted for nuns from the friars' constitutions. First, we have the *Rule of San Sisto*, taken probably from the first *Customs* adopted by

---

[5] Vicaire, op.cit., p. 429-430

[6] Creytens, op. cit.

the friars in 1216.[7] Then come the *Statutes* of the Penitents, taken from the primitive *Constitutions* of the friars, as drawn up in 1220 and 1221, and further refined in 1228. After that come the *Constitutions of Montargis*, drawn up for that monastery c. 1250 and taken, as Creytens has shown,[8] from the friars' constitutions as they were redacted by Raymund of Penyafort, third Master of the Order. Finally, we have the *Constitutions* promulgated by Humbert of Romans in 1259, which are based on the legislation of the friars as it stood at that time. These remained the standard for the nuns until the 19th century, although they were printed in tandem with the friars' constitutions and were meant to evolve in all particulars that could apply to the nuns, just as the friars' constitutions evolved.

I wish to thank all those who helped me with the obscurities of medieval

---

[7] Vicaire, op.cit., p. 433-434

[8] Creytens, op. cit.

Latin, including Fr. Roger Landry and Fr. Chrysogonus Waddell, O.C.S.O. and my own sisters in community. These assisted me with not only practical but also moral support. Special thanks are due to the late Sr. Maria of the Cross, O.P. who reviewed the entire manuscript and made many helpful suggestions. May her soul rejoice in the Presence of God forever!

Now, after eighteen more years have elapsed, we are reprinting this translation. I continue to view it as a labor of love and as a "service of renewal and adaptation," a way of keeping us nuns in touch with our roots.

Sr. Mary Martin Jacobs, O.P.
July 22, 2022

INSTITUTES OF THE SISTERS OF SAN SISTO OF ROME

INTRODUCTION to the Latin Edition

By Andre Simon

Independently of the text transcribed in the registers of Nicholas IV (v.p. 30 & R.44 and R.169) which we have not been able to consult, the same Pope's original Bull in the archives at Breslau (v.R. 169) preserves an authenticated copy, *which we are using as a basis for the edition of our text.* A few passages have become illegible due to the age of the parchment. However, since an authenticated copy of this document was made in 1305 for the convent of the Penitents of Malchow in Mecklenburg, we have been able to restore the text of the worn passages without any trouble, thanks to the copy obligingly furnished us by the archivist Dr. Grotefend.

The different editions of these *Institutes* agree with each other very closely, and the variants presented create no serious difficulties for understanding the text itself. Nevertheless, we will indicate the different readings.[9] These are the editions we are dealing with:

1) DUELLIUS, *Miscellaneorum T.*I, p. 169-180, from a manuscript of the Bibliotheque Dorotheenne, today at the Hofbibliothek of Vienna, Cod. 4724, fol. 311-317. This gives the text of the Bull of Gregory IX.
2) BREMOND, *Bullarium Ord. Praed.*, VII, p. 410-413, gives the complete Bull of Gregory IX (v.R.44). The editor mentions a copy from the Archives of the

---

[9] Andre Simon's critical apparatus is omitted in this translation, since, for the most part, it has no meaning apart from the Latin text.

Order of Preachers, itself made from an exemplar in the Vatican archives. This cannot refer to Gregory IX's Registers, which do not contain it, but rather to those of Nicholas IV, or to a copy specially made from his Registers. The editor of the *Bullarium* is familiar with the Duellius edition, and their texts agree with each other consistently. Their common source seems to be the same Bull of Gregory IX.

3) M*ecklenburg. Urkunden-Buch,* III, p. 402, contains several extracts from the Bull of Nicholas IV, following the *Vidimu*s of Malchow.

4) ERMISCH, *Urkunden-Buch der Stadt Freiburg,* I, n. 605, reproduces the entire Bull of Gregory IX with the text of the *Institutes,* from the Breslau original (R. 169) and the *Vidinus* of Malchow.

5) BALME, *Cartulaire de St. Dominique,* III, p. 425-453, edited the Bull of Nicholas IV. He knows of the existence of the Duellius, Bremond and *Meckl. U.B.* editions, as well as the text in the registers of Nicholas IV and that of the *Vidimus* of Malchow; but he does not explain how he established his text.
6) The *Analecta Ordinis Fr. Praedicatorum*, III, p. 628-635 reproduces the entire Bull of Gregory IX and indicates the same sources as Balme, following his edition without any comparison of texts.

Chapter and paragraph titles have been added by the editor.

INSTITUTES OF THE SISTERS OF SAN SISTO OF ROME

Index of Chapters

PROLOGUE

1. Just as in the very beginning of the new-born Church, the multitude of believers was of one heart and one mind, and held everything in common,[10] so you ought to have one set of customs and one manner of life in the house of the Lord. It is likewise fitting that you, who live under the same rule and the one profession of vows, should always be found uniform in the norms for living the life and in the observances of canonical religion, which are as follows:

I. RECEIVING SISTERS

1. Whoever is received into the sisterhood shall promise obedience, stability in the place and in the Order, to live without anything of her own, and also continently. No one is to go out of the

---

[10] Acts, 4:32; Rule of St. Augustine, chapter 1

house in which she has made profession, unless she is transferred to another convent of the same Order for a necessary reason.

2. The norms for living the life are as follows:

II. MEALS

1. From the feast of the Lord's Resurrection until the feast of the Holy Cross in September, the sisters may eat twice a day, 2. except Fridays, Rogation days, the vigil of Pentecost and the fasts of the Ember days, the vigils of Sts. John the Baptist, Peter and Paul, James, Lawrence, the Assumption of the Blessed Mary, and St. Bartholomew. 3. From the feast of the Holy Cross in September until Easter, they may eat once a day, except for Sundays, unless someone is sick or infirm, or has been dispensed for some other reason.

III. QUALITY AND QUANTITY OF FOOD

1. Each day, if possible, they are to have two cooked dishes; the prioress, however, can add to this, insofar as she judges it to be expedient and the resources of the house permit. 2. Throughout Advent and Lent, as well as during the fast of the Ember days, the vigils of Ascension, Pentecost, the apostles and other saints on whose vigils fasting is indicated, and on all Fridays, the sisters are to eat Lenten fare. 3. On those days, the sisters who serve are not to take the *mixtum.*[11] 4. In the refectory, there is always to be reading at the meals and the sisters are to listen to the reading in attentive silence.

---

[11] The *mixtum was* most probably a little bread and diluted wine. cf. *Ecclesiastica Officia* (Cistercian Customs), Chap. LXXIII. The most convenient edition is Daniele Choisselet - Placide Vernet, *Les Ecclesiastica Officia cisterciens du XIIeme siecle.* Documentation cistercienne 22 (Reiningue, France; 1989, p. 216

IV. THE SICK

1. By all means, let the prioress be careful concerning the sick, that she not be negligent or over-austere; rather, the sick are to be provided for in such a way that they may recover more speedily. 2. Let flesh meat be allowed to the sick, feeble and elderly in the infirmary, as the Rule of the blessed Benedict permits.[12] If someone has an infirmity that weakens her only a little and does not interfere with her appetite, she should not use it as a pretext to sleep on a mattress, or break the customary fasts, or change her food in the refectory. 4. Let her read and work as the prioress enjoins her.

V. COLLATION

1. After vespers, let all come together for the collation, where there should be reading, as is customary in the

---

[12] Rule of Benedict, Chap. XXXVI

Cistercian Order.[13]

VI. THE RECEPTION OF YOUNG GIRLS

1. It is not our custom to receive young girls under the age of eleven. 2. If, however, some are received at a younger age in order to save them from grave scandal or for their spiritual welfare, they should be brought up in a place apart and diligently formed in good behavior until the age of fourteen. 3. Furthermore, the sick, the convalescent and young girls ought not to be burdened with abstinence or fasts.

VII. SILENCE

1. Let the sisters keep silence everywhere in the house, except in the parlor and in the chapter hall at the time of

---

[13] *Ecclesiastica Officia* (Cistercian Customs), Chap. LXXXI; Choisselet - Vernet, p. 232-235

chapter, and let them not speak even in the parlor without special permission. 2. In the work room they may speak silently about those things which pertain to the work, and also at the window with the permission of the prioress. 3. Indeed, the prioress can occasionally give permission to speak in other places for reasons of necessity or usefulness, and she herself may also speak when she judges it expedient.

VIII. CLOTHING

1. Let the clothing which you will wear be white, and not too finely woven or delicate, lest your habit attract attention, for you ought not to please others by your clothing, but by your manner of life and the purity of your mind, because the glory of the King's daughter should be from within.[14] 2. It should suffice for the nuns to have two tunics and two thick knee-length

---

[14] Ps. 45:14; Rule of St. Augustine, chapter 4

undergarments, made with suitable pelts. The tunic is not to go below the heel, nor drag unbecomingly on the ground. Each sister may have two mantles, if her house is prosperous enough to afford it, one of which is made with pelts, as well as a scapular, the necessary footwear, and two veils.

IX. BEDS AND BEDDING

1. Each sister will sleep on straw covered with wool, in a woolen garment, and an undergarment if she wishes, but always with a belt.

X. THE TONSURE

1. The nuns and the friars, including the lay brothers, should have their hair tonsured. eight times a year, that is to say: at Easter, Pentecost, the feasts of the blessed apostles Peter and Paul, and St. Mary Magdalene, on the Nativity of the

Blessed Virgin, the feast of All Saints, the Nativity of the Lord and the Purification of the glorious Virgin

XI. LIGHTER FAULTS

1. These are lighter faults: 2. If anyone has offended her sisters, she shall prostrate herself at her feet until the other, placated, raises her up, unless she was so upset that it is impossible to soothe her even with lengthy entreaties. Nevertheless, the offended one must not afterward avoid the punishment due her hardness of heart. 3. If anyone did not have a definite task which she absolutely had to carry out, and, as soon as the signal was given, she neglected to leave off everything else and prepare herself to say the Hours according to the rule in an orderly and peaceful manner, or to fulfill becomingly her designated role as reader or singer. 4. If, when intoning a responsory or antiphon, anyone disturbed the choir by reading or

singing in a disorderly manner and the offender did not immediately humble herself in the presence of all. 5. If she negligently put off going to her work at the time when work is to be done. 6. If while at work she heedlessly made some loud noise or disturbance. 7. If she did not come to table with the others at the appointed hour. 8. If she was not present for the common tonsuring. 9. If she made some disturbance in the dormitory. 10. If she spilled her drink. 11. If she said or did anything by which her sisters were offended. 12. If perhaps she made some reprehensible gesture or attracted attention to herself in anything. 13. If she took drink or food without a blessing. 14. If she disturbed those who were working or has herself performed her work idly. 15. If, when she had permission to speak, she laughed carelessly and by loud laughter or joking words or deeds deliberately intended to excite others to laughter. 16. If she was not present for the *Glory to the Father* of the first psalm and did not immediately make satisfaction at the altar step. 17. For each of these faults a psalm is to be imposed as a penance on the one seeking pardon.

XII. MEDIUM FAULTS

1. The following are examples of a medium fault: 2. If anyone laughed openly in choir or made others laugh. 3. If she did not come to chapter or the Office. 4. If she affirmed or denied anything with an oath, as is customary in speaking. 5. If, when she had permission to speak, she said something obscene. 6. If she broke the prescribed silence. 7. If any of the sisters who is assigned to an office was found negligent in anything regarding that office and did not correct herself after two warnings. 8. If she took clothing or anything else given to another sister without the consent of that sister or the permission of the prioress. 9. A sister who

has been proclaimed in chapter for any of the above-mentioned faults should ask pardon and receive a moderate discipline, with as many psalms as it pleases the one who will preside at chapter.

XII. A GRAVE FAULT

1. The following are examples of a grave fault: 2. If anyone, through obstinacy or open rebellion was disobedient to her prioress or had a quarrel with her prelate,[15] prioress or subprioress. 3. If she fought disgracefully with a sister. 4. If she spoke with some person outside the community without permission or contrary to the laws of the Order. 5. If, in passing before men, she stared at them intentionally[16] and made a habit of this. 6. If she was caught telling a deliberate lie. 7. If she broke silence habitually. 8. If she presumed to sow

[15] *prelato,* i.e. male superior

[16] Literally, *fixed her eyes*; cf. Rule of St. Augustine, chapter 4

discord between friars and sisters. 9. If she was caught maliciously uttering threats, curses or even irreligious words against a sister who proclaimed her at chapter, or against anyone else. 10. If she dared to reproach any sister for a past fault for which she had made satisfaction, or if she revealed the secrets of the chapter. 11. If she said something bad about the friars, sisters, or her superiors, which she is not able to prove by the testimony of her sisters. 12. If she conversed alone with a man,[17] except the confessor. 13. For these and similar faults, if she has sought pardon and not been proclaimed, three disciplines are to be given in chapter and three days of fast on bread and water are to be imposed on her, but not three consecutive days. If, however, she was proclaimed, another discipline and an extra day of fast are to be added, 14. If, however, she has presumed to murmur about the

---

[17] *sola cum solo*

food or clothing or anything else, rather than choose to expose her needs or lack first to the (male) superior or to the prioress, and failed in this many times, she must undergo the above-mentioned punishment, and for forty days she is to be forced to do without the kind of food, drink or other object about which she has murmured.

XIV. A VERY GRAVE FAULT

1. The following are examples of a very grave fault: 2. If anyone deliberately struck another, or committed a deadly crime, such as theft, sacrilege or anything of that sort, or deliberately hid something which had been donated to her personally or to the community. 3. If her fault was public and she has been proclaimed in chapter, she should spontaneously get up, humbly beg pardon and confess her fault. Afterwards, on her bare flesh she shall receive the discipline in proportion to her

deeds. 4. Since graver faults are worthy of a more enduring penance, let her receive precepts such as: she is to be last of all the sisters in the community for a time, so that, as she was not ashamed to become a member of the devil by committing this fault, she may now be confounded and sorrowful in the sight of all the sisters for an appropriate period of time, thus bearing worthy fruits of penitence. 5. In the refectory, she will not sit at the common table with the rest, but will eat in the middle of the refectory upon a bare table. 6. Coarse bread will be provided for her separately and water to drink, unless the prioress should grant her something else out of compassion. 7. The remains of her meal are not to be mixed with that of the others, so that she may realize that, just as she is separated from the companionship of her sisters on earth, so she will be deprived forever of the fellowship of the saints, unless through worthy penitence she again becomes a member of Christ. 8. She may come to the canonical Hours but must remain at the entrance of the church, lying prostrate as the sisters pass by, until everyone has entered. 9. No one is to dare associate with her or command her to do anything. 10. Nevertheless, so that she may not fall into despair, let the prioress herself send some of the older and more prudent sisters to her. These ought to admonish her to do penance and stir her to grief, support her by their compassion and encourage her to make satisfaction. Let them aid her by their prayers of intercession, which they must not omit to pour out for her continually, 11. Furthermore, if they see in her signs of humility and repentance, let the whole community support her; nor may the prioress refuse to have mercy on her when she sees that it is expedient. 12. When it is time for her to be reconciled, let her throw herself at the feet of all, seeking the mercy, first of the prioress, and then, from there, of the sisters seated on either side. 13. During such time as she is performing this penance, she should not receive Communion, except in danger of death, nor come for the kiss of peace, since she is separated from the company of her sisters. 14. If she had been prioress or some other official, she is to be deprived of her office in perpetuity, nor may she afterward be given another office, unless she is dispensed through a general chapter. 15. If a sin of this kind was secret, the sister must endeavor to make satisfaction to God by secret and discreet penance, appropriate to the time and person, as she has been commanded. 16. If anyone presumed openly to rebel against her male or female superiors by conspiracy or plot, 17. or if anyone deliberately slandered the friars or sisters or her superiors in front of outsiders, or maliciously complained to her parents or others about any affair contrary to the laws of the Order, from which scandal could arise, let her do penance in the above-mentioned manner. 18. Besides, for her whole life, she must take the last place in rank, 19. nor may any administrative post be assigned to her, except by the major superior or through a general chapter, if it should grant her a dispensation. 20. If, however, she has observed something against a male or female superior, not maliciously but in truth, which ought not or cannot be tolerated, let her first endeavor to admonish such a person with all humility and charity for her correction. 21. If, after frequent admonitions, the superior has neglected or disdained to correct herself, the sister should inform the prior of the house, so that the person may be admonished and corrected. Or let her take care to inform the guardians when they come to visitate the church. Or she may endeavor to notify the major superior or the general chapter.

XV. THE MOST GRAVE FAULT

1. The most grave fault is incorrigibility, because one does not fear to admit faults and refuses to undergo penance. 2. Such a person should be incarcerated, whipped, and placed under the penalty described above for very grave faults, until she makes appropriate satisfaction. 3. Nevertheless, the major superior has the freedom and power to decrease or increase the punishment. 4. Nuns who have left once out of levity of spirit should never again be re admitted, except by the special mercy of the major superior of the Order.

XVI. WINDOWS

1. Three of the more mature and religious sisters are to be put in charge of the parlor windows, so that they, or at least two of them, might listen to a sister who is speaking there, whenever the prior or

prioress has given someone permission to speak, as it seems good to them. 2. A guardian (male) of the windows is also to be present at all times and should make every effort to watch the words and gestures of those who are speaking. 3. If he has heard anything less than modest or discreet, or contrary to religion, he is immediately to impose silence on the speakers and take care to report to the prioress or prior as soon as possible. 4. A fitting penance should be imposed on the delinquent and her permission to speak should be suspended, according to the gravity of the fault and as the prioress sees fit. 5. However, the prioress and three cellarers can speak at the window with the prior and extern cellarers about matters that are necessary and useful to the house, so long as the above-mentioned witnesses are present.

XVII. ENCLOSURE

1. None of the friars is to enter the enclosure of the nuns, except in the company of a cardinal, bishop, or legate of the Apostolic See, or in cases permitted in this rule. 2. Once inside, he is not to speak with any nun, unless he does this with the permission of the major superior or prior provincial. 3. However, the prior provincial may enter once a year, at the time of visitation, unless the master general[18] makes provision for some other necessity. 4. If a sister is not able to go to the window to confess, receive Communion, or be anointed for a grave illness, a priest and mature ministers may enter, clothed in sacred vestments, to perform these functions, but they are not to speak of anything else. 5. Whenever anyone enters for some necessary reason, he is to have

---

[18] *preposito generali*

with him no fewer than two [male] companions of good repute, and three of the more religious nuns are to follow them, keeping them always in view, until they leave the nuns' enclosure. 6. With the permission of the prioress, the nuns may speak with the [male] guardian of the windows concerning the necessary business of the house. 7. Furthermore, the nuns in charge of the windows are not to make a habit of asking permission to speak to the guardian when he is on duty; without the permission of the prioress they are not to speak to outsiders. 8. By custom, danger from robbers and fire absolves completely from both fault and penalty those entering and speaking. 9. If the need arises, the bursars may speak a few words about figs with the one who cultivates them, if this gardener is a man about whom not the slightest suspicion could arise. 10. If a sister has spoken with any man other than the ones mentioned here, unless he is a cardinal, bishop, or legate, or even responds to a question unless she has permission to reply, let her undergo the penalty due for a grave fault, until she is absolved by the major superior.

XVIII. THE GOODS OF THE MONASTERY

1. The prior and extern cellarers shall not dare to sell or give away the external goods of the monastery, whether gold or silver or clothing or anything else, without the permission of the major superior, unless by the advice and consent of the prioress and sister-cellarers. 2. Similarly, the internal possessions, situated within the house, cannot be exchanged or reduced without the consent of the chapter or the master general. 3. Both the internal and external officials are to render an account of receipts and expenses before the prior or master general twice a year, or more frequently if this should be required. 4. In

addition, they should make an accounting to the prioress and the more mature nuns, at least three of them, as often as it seems expedient.

XIX. THE CHANGING OF PERSONNEL

1. If any sisters should come to another convent of the same Order with testimonial letters from the master general or prior provincial, let them be received kindly, 2. and let them be assigned to a place in the refectory and dormitory along with the rest of the sisters. 3. However, no one, either cleric or lay brother or sister, may dare to receive or dismiss a friar or sister without a mandate from the master general or one to whom he has delegated his powers. But the male superior has the power of removing clerics, lay seculars and the bursars of the sisters, when he sees fit.

XX. WORK

1. For the rest, since idleness is the enemy of the soul and the mother and nurse of vices, let no one in the cloister remain idle; but let each one always be doing some work, because she who occupies herself with good activity is not easily ensnared by temptation. 2. For it was said to the man by the LORD that by the sweat of his face he ought to earn his bread;[19] and the Apostle says: “If someone will not work, let him not eat;”[20] and the prophet: "By the labors of your hands you shall eat. Happy are you and it shall go well for you."[21] 3. Therefore, with the exception of those hours which ought to be dedicated to prayer, reading, or preparation for the divine office or chant, or the study of letters, let all devote themselves attentively

---

[19] Gen 3:19

[20] II Thess 3:10

[21] Ps 128:2

to some manual labor, as the prioress sees fit.

XXI. READING AND PRAYER

1. Let the hebdomadarians prepare the texts which they must read or sing. 2. On feast days, let all the nuns devote themselves to reading, the divine office, and prayer, putting aside all mechanical work, 3. After Compline and the Nocturns, the sisters will have one hour during which they may devote themselves to prayer, contemplation and devotion; nevertheless, let no one disturb the others by coming late to the dormitory. 4. On ferial days, all without exception should continue to attend the canonical hours with devotion. On these days Prime, Terce, Sext and None may be said in the workroom, if this seems advisable.

XXII. AVOIDING HASTY JUDGMENTS

1. Let each and all be diligently on guard not to presume in any way to persecute with rancor or hatred, or to disturb even slightly with calumnies or quarreling or unjust accusations a faithful nun who would reprove or resist those who do things contrary to religion or the constitutions of the Order, 2. or who would report transgressions to the prioress, prior, or major superior, that they may be corrected according to the rule. 3. If anyone would presume to act otherwise, let them undergo to the last degree the penalty for a grave fault, so that the rest may watch themselves and not presume to do similar things.

XXIII. THE BROTHER AND SISTER BURSARS

1. In every house of this Order there should be appointed, if they are

available, four God-fearing male religious who will procure external goods. 2. In the same way, four nuns are to be internal bursars, who will procure everything according to the counsel of the prior and prioress. 3. These, however, are not to presume to give away gold, silver, clothing, grain or anything else without the permission of the prior or prioress.

XXIV. ELECTIONS

1. The prioress shall be elected by some of the older and more prudent sisters of the community, chosen for this purpose by the community; 2. and she shall be confirmed by the master general, by whom she can also be removed from office when he sees fit. 3. The other officials ought to be appointed and changed by the prioress, with the advice of the older and more prudent sisters, in all things safeguarding the provision and mandate of the master general. 4. In the same way, the prior is to

be elected by his brethren; however, he is to be confirmed, or if necessary, designated and appointed, by the master general.

XXV. THE RULE OF THE FRIARS

1. The friars should observe the rule of Blessed Augustine. 2. In any house there are to be at least six friars, religious professed according to the rule of Blessed Augustine, of whom at least three are to be ordained priests.

STATUTES OF THE SISTERS OF SAINT MARY MAGDALENE

STATUTES OF THE SISTERS OF SAINT MARY MAGDALENE

INTRODUCTION to the Latin Edition

By Andre Simon

As basis for our edition we have used the only extant text, preserved in *Cod. Lat.* 4724 (fol. 320-328v) in the Hofbibliothek of Vienna, edited by DUELLIUS, *Miscell.* I, p. 182-198. This author, unfamiliar with the primitive Constitutions of the Preachers and unaware that our Statutes depend closely upon that Dominican legislation, was not in a position to compare the texts with his version, which is sometimes defective. We have been able to correct the errors in doubtful passages by going back to the texts of these *Consuetudin*es, or primitive Constitutions, as edited by DENIFLE, *Archiv*. I, p. 165-227.

Two 18th Century German translations of the Statutes exist, which are still in force [c. 1918] in the convents of Lauban and Studenitz. [*Regelbuch,* v.D.IV, note.] They present several slight variants to our text, and supplementary notes which indicate a more recent original source. However, they have enabled us to restore our text in several doubtful places; and we have not hesitated to do this whenever they agreed with the text of the primitive Constitutions of the Preachers.

Comparative examination of our sources allows us to assign, with quasi-certitude, the editing of the Statutes to the year 1232 at the latest. It was in that year that the Penitents received from the hands of the pope the Institutes of San Sisto and the first Constitutions of the Dominicans, which are none other than these Statutes.

STATUTES OF THE SISTERS OF SAINT MARY MAGDALENE

Index of Chapters

This index was compiled by the editor.

Here begin the Constitutions of the Sisters of Saint Mary Magdalene

I. THE DIVINE OFFICE

1. On hearing the first signal for Matins, the sisters should get up, while reciting Matins of the Blessed Virgin.

2. Inclinations. When that is finished and the sisters have entered choir, let them make a profound inclination before the altar. When they have gone to their seats, at a signal from the prioress they should say the *Our Father* and *Apostles' Creed,* either kneeling or making a profound inclination; when the prioress gives the signal again, they should arise. 3. Having thus devoutly begun the Hour, let them turn to the altar and arm themselves with the Sign of the Cross; and at the *Glory to the Father* let them make a profound inclination choir to choir or prostrate themselves according to the day, until the words *as it was in the beginning.*

4. This is to be done whenever the *Our Father* and *Apostles' Creed* are said, except during Mass and before the readings and during the graces after meals. 5. However, the incli-nation or prostration is to be done at the first collect in the Mass and at the post-communion prayer, and likewise at prayers for the Church and at each Hour during the collect and at the *Glory to the Father* whenever it is said at the beginning of an Hour. 6. At every *Glory to the Father,* at the last verse of the hymns and at the penultimate verse of the canticle *Bless the Lord (the Canticle of the Three Youths), we* make the inclination all the way to the knees. When *Glory to God* is sung, we incline at the words *receive our prayer,* and during the Creed in the Mass at the words *and became man,* as well as at the blessing before the readings. Likewise, we do this during the prayer at Chapter *Holy Mary*, etc. and in every prayer when the name of the blessed Mary is mentioned and of Mary

Magdalene. 7. At the *Hail Holy Mother* and the *Come Holy Spirit,* we kneel. 8. On ferial days, we lie prostrate from the *Holy, Holy, Holy,* all the way to the *Lamb of God*; on feasts of three readings or nine, we prostrate from the elevation of the Body of Christ all the way to the *Our Father.* 9. We observe the same prostrations on feasts of three or nine readings, except that on a feast of three readings we omit the prostration at Vespers. We also omit it on feasts of nine readings at the preceding None, except during Lent; then we prostrate at None of the vigil and likewise on the feast itself during the Mass of Lent.

10. Having begun the Hour in the aforementioned way [I, 1-3), after they have made the inclination at the *Glory to the Father* which ends the psalm *Come, ring out our joy* [Ps. 95), let them stand choir to choir. At the first psalm, let one choir sit; at the second psalm, let them stand and the other choir sit, and they should thus

alternate up to the psalm *Praise the Lord from the heavens* [Ps. 148]. Let them do the same at all the Hours.

11. Chapter is held at the end of Matins or after Prime, as the prioress sees fit. 12. For entering chapter and also for going up to communion, this order is kept: those in authority precede and the other sisters follow in rank.

II. CHAPTER

1. When the community has entered chapter, let the reader first announce the lunar day and whatever is to be read out from the Calendar; then let the hebdomadarian say: *Precious in the eyes of the Lord,* etc. 2. The sisters sit down and the reader reads from the rule or the constitutions, prefacing it with: *Lady, give the blessing*; and the hebdomadarian intones

the blessing: *Regularibus disciplinis*[22] or *May the divine assistance remain always with us,* according to the day. 3. After absolution for the dead has been given, the one who presides at chapter should say*: Bless*; and let everyone make an inclination, responding *the Lord.* 4. Then a list of benefactions received is read out and the prioress says *Be pleased, Lord, to repay with eternal life* etc. The community should also say the psalms *To you have I lifted up my* eyes [Ps. 123] and *Out of the depths* [Ps. 130] for the dead, followed by *Lord have mercy, Christ have mercy, Lord have mercy, Our Father* and the three versicles: *Let us pray for the Lord Pope; Save your servants, O Lord; May they rest in peace.* The hebdomadarian should then say these three collects: *Almighty, eternal God; Stretch out, Lord, the right hand; O God,*

---

[22] It has proven impossible for me to find the full text of this blessing. It may never have made it into the definitive liturgical texts of the Order edited in 1245. Almost all the other prayers were still current before Vatican II.

creator and redeemer of all the faithful. Then the sisters may sit down again. 5. After this, the prioress may speak briefly about whatever she judges necessary for their upbuilding or correction. 6. She should end with: *Let us speak for our good.* 7. Then let those who have failed in anything arise and prostrate themselves, seeking pardon. 8. After that, they humbly get up and confess their faults. 9. And if anyone's fault is such that it is worthy of correction,[23] let them prepare themselves for correction, which the prioress will administer, or someone whom she has delegated.

9a. In chapter, the sisters are not to speak except for two reasons: to state simply their own or another's faults and to respond to the prioress' questions.[24] 10. The sisters are in no way to proclaim someone in

---

[23] i.e., the discipline

[24] This number was inserted by the editor from the Rodez manuscript of the friars' constitutions.

chapter on suspicion alone. 11. Whenever the prioress has imposed some prayer, let all make an inclination; similarly, all should do this whenever she has commanded them to say or do anything. 12. If she has imposed any office or obedience on someone, let the sister humbly prostrate herself, receiving what has been laid upon her. 13. After the faults have been heard, the psalm is said: *Praise the Lord all you nations* (Ps. 117], with the verse: *Lord, show us your mercy* and *Lord, hear my prayer*, with the collect: *Direct, O Lord, our actions.* 14. Finally, the prioress shall say: *Our help is in the name of the Lord,* and thus chapter is ended.

15. Let the prioress beware lest the silence or peace of the sisters be interrupted or impeded by the administration of temporal affairs. 16. Therefore, a place shall always be designated where the prioress may speak with the officials, or the officials among themselves, whenever necessary, so

that those who wish to give themselves up to prayer and contemplation may be in no way impeded. 17. Let no one presume to quarrel with her prioress.

III. THE MAINTENANCE OF THE ENCLOSURE

1. Let the enclosure be shut and guarded with steadfast and most diligent watchfulness so that no place may be given to the devil. 2. The window where the sisters may converse with their friends when they come to visit them must be most firmly closed with iron grilles and bars. 3. A doorkeeper will be assigned to this window, whose duty will be to report to the prioress which sisters would speak at the window and to whom, so that she may give permission or not, at her discretion. 4. Let none of the sisters presume to go to the window without special permission and without a companion assigned to her. 5. The prioress must be careful always to

assign more mature companions to the younger sisters. And let everyone beware, not only the doorkeeper and the companion, but the other sisters as well, lest they scandalize seculars, whether by word or deed or any irreligious gesture, or by showing levity of mind, and thus make themselves contemptible and defame the Order. 6. No one is to speak to outsiders, except in the hearing of her nearby companion. 7. However, a large window can be made in the same way so that the word of the Lord can be preached there. 8. Also, two small windows of similar form may be put in the church, if possible, where the confessions of the sisters shall be heard. 9. In every opening, grilles are to be made such that a hen's egg cannot be passed through; and they are to have long, sharp spikes facing outward and inward. 10. Men are never to enter into the cloister, workshops, or oratory of the sisters, except a priest to hear the confessions of the sick, to give them Communion, and to anoint them, or a doctor or an architect when it is necessary for their work; 11. and this only under the witness of three persons whom the prioress shall appoint. 12. Women also are not to enter, unless the sisters have a very great need for their help. This need is to be determined with the counsel of the older and more mature nuns. 13. Whether men or women, when the task for which they were summoned is completed, they are to leave immediately.

IV. THE OFFICE OF THE CHURCH

1. Let our sisters hear Matins and all the Hours together, and eat together, unless the prioress wishes to arrange otherwise for some of the sisters. 2. All the Hours are to be said in the church, succinctly and briefly lest the sisters lose devotion and their work be impeded in the least. We say that the Office is to be done

in this manner: that in the middle of the psalm verses, a mediant[25] is to be observed with a pause, not drawing out the voice at the pause nor at the end of the verse. But as was said above, it should be ended briefly and succinctly; and this is to be done in varying degrees according to the season. 3. Sisters who do not know the choral Office and do not have the ability to learn it, may say their Hours silently by themselves in this way: At Matins, having said the *Our Father* and *Apostles' Creed,* let them say *O Lord, open my lips, O God, come to my assistance; Glory to the Father*, then the Nocturn and Lauds. 4. On ferial days, let them say the Nocturn according to the feria, and Lauds according to the feria. After the *Blessed be the Lord, the God of Israel* (Canticle of Zechariah], let them say *Lord, have mercy, Christ have mercy, Lord have mercy, Our Father, And lead us not into*

---

[25] The mediant is a brief silence between halves of a psalm verse, usually the space of a breath.

temptation; Through Our Lord Jesus Christ; Let us bless the Lord; Thanks be to God. 5. On Sundays and feasts of nine readings, let them say the Nocturn of the day, with these psalms of Lauds: *The Lord is king* [Ps. 92]; *Cry out with joy to the Lord* [Ps. 99]; etc. 6. At Prime on Sundays, let them say: My *God, My God, why have you forsaken me?* [Ps. 22], up to: *The Lord is my light* [Ps. 27]; after that, *O God, save me by your name* [Ps. 54]; *They are happy whose life is blameless* [Ps. 119,1]; *Bless your servant and I shall live* [Ps. 119, 17]; and the *Athanasian Creed* [*Quicumque vult*]. After the psalms, let them say: *Lord have mercy, Christ have mercy, Lord have mercy; Our Father,* etc., as above. 7. Let them do the same at the other Hours, saying the psalms which are assigned to each Hour, and after the psalms, *Lord have mercy,* etc. 8. With regard to inclinations and prostrations, let them conform to the sisters singing in the choir.

V. MEALS

[Concerning meals] and the regular fasts, let everything that is contained in the rule be observed without violation [Chap. II].

VI. THE MANNER OF GOING TO DINNER

1. At the hour appointed for dinner or supper, the sacristan is to ring the bell a few strokes so that the sisters may not be late in coming to the refectory. 2. Then a gong is sounded, if the food is prepared; otherwise, let it not be sounded until the food is ready. 3. When they have washed their hands, the prioress strikes the little refectory bell and the sisters enter. 4. When they have entered, she begins by ringing the small bell; when it has been rung, let the one who says the versicles say *Bless the Lord*; then the community should proceed to say the graces and eat. 5. Let the prioress sit in

the middle of the table and the others choir to choir on both sides of her. 6. The reader will receive the blessing in her place. 7. The servers should begin with the prioress, and so on down to the juniors.[26]

8. Except for the servers, no sister is to stay away from the first table unless she has permission; and whoever has stayed away shall eat at the second table, so that there is no need for a third table. 9. There is to be no allowance of food for the servers or helpers which is not given to the community, unless the prioress should find it expedient to treat them otherwise. 10. The prioress shall eat in the refectory; likewise the infirmarians and the helpers and the other sisters, unless the prioress shall dispense some, for whatever reason, so

[26] The primitive constitutions of the friars, the constitutions redacted by Raymond of Penyafort, and the constitutions drawn up for the nuns of the Order by Humbert of Romans all have the reverse order: *let then begin with the juniors and proceed up to the prior's table.*

that they may eat apart from the community. 11. If, however, the prioress should become ill, let her obtain her food in the infirmary, along with the other sisters. 12. No sister shall send some food to another sister, except the prioress; from the portion given to her she can give to those on her right and left.

VII. FOOD

1. Everywhere in our convents the food should be without meat. 2. But our friars and lay brothers may eat food cooked with meat when out of the cloister, except in our *curias*, in order not to be a burden to people. 3. In the same way, our friars are not to presume to eat outside of their convent or *curia* in places where they have one, unless it happens to be with the bishop, and that rarely. 4. Every day they (the nuns) are to have two cooked dishes, if possible. The prioress, however, can add another dish whenever she wants and as she

sees fit, whether for herself or others, in order to support the weak. Thus she may serve in some way either herself or other sick sisters, now to these, now to those. 5. Also, if the convent itself does not have an abundance of wine because of a lack of resources, just as the prioress may increase the dishes, we allow her to have verjuice[27] or mead or beer at her own table. 6. If anyone should see that someone sitting next to her lacks anything that was served to the community, let her ask it from the cellarer or server. 7. If any of the servers or those eating should commit some offense in serving or eating, let her arise immediately and seek pardon; and, at a signal given by the prioress, let her return to her place. 8. Whoever wishes to drink outside the appointed hour should ask

[27] *Vinum terre,* translation conjectural. Verjuice is a sour drink made from the juice of unripe fruit such as crab apples or green grapes.

permission and take a companion.

VIII. COLLATION

1. During the fasting season, at the appointed hour the sacristan rings a signal; and when the sisters are gathered in community, at a signal from the prioress, the reader reads, beginning with: *Lady, give the blessing*, and the blessing follows: *May the almighty and merciful Lord grant us a quiet night and eternal life.* 2. During the reading, after the prioress has given the signal and the reader has said *Bless the Lord* and the hebdomadarian has given the blessing: *May the giver of all good things bless the drink of his servants*, the sisters may drink. 3. When the reading is finished, let the one who presides say: *Our help is in the name of the Lord*; and then, in silence, they shall all enter the church. 4. During other seasons, before Compline this lesson is read in the church: *Brethren, be sober,* etc., and after the confession has been made and

Compline said, let the one who presides give the blessing. After this, the *Our Father* and *Apostles' Creed* are said. This also is to be done before Prime and Matins.

X. BEDS

1. Our sisters are not to sleep on mattresses, except for the sick. 2. They are to sleep in a belted tunic. 3. They will be allowed to sleep on straw and on woolen mats and sacking.

X. THE SICK

1. Let the prioress beware lest she neglect the sick; everything must be obtained for them that will enable them to recover speedily. 2. They may even eat meat if the gravity of their illness requires it, as the prioress sees fit. 3. If someone has an illness that neither weakens her too much nor disturbs her appetite, such as a swelling or cut on the limbs or anything of that sort,

she is not for that reason to lie on a mattress or break the customary fast or change from the food in the refectory. 4. Let her work as her prioress enjoins her.

XI. BLOODLETTING

1. Bloodletting is to take place four times a year: First, in the month of September; second, after Christmas; third, after Easter; fourth, around the feast of John the Baptist. 2. Outside of these times, no one is to presume to have her blood let, except at the discretion of the prioress for some reason which she has judged necessary. 3. Those whose blood is being let should eat outside the refectory, in a place where this can be conveniently attended to; and they are to be provided for in greater abundance, as the resources of the house permit. 4. Bloodletting is not an excuse for them to eat meat.

XII. THE INSTRUCTION OF NOVICES

1. The prioress shall appoint one of the more mature and upright sisters as mistress over those who are received as novices, and she shall teach them about the Order. 2. Wherever they behave negligently, let her strive to correct them, by word or sign, insofar as possible. 3. She should also proclaim them frequently before the prioress in chapter for their public negligences. 4. Let her teach them to have humility of heart and body and strive to form them in this very thing, according to the text: *Learn of me, for I am meek and humble of heart* (Mt. 11:29). 5. She shall teach them to confess frequently, simply and with discretion, to have nothing of their own, to surrender their self-will for the sake of the prioress' will, and to observe voluntary obedience everywhere and in all things. 6. Let her instruct them how to

behave becomingly everywhere; to remain in the place where they are assigned; 7. how to make the inclinations; 8. how they should keep to their quarters, behaving modestly, not with eyes upraised, but with their heads hidden in their capuces; 9. how or what they should pray for and how to do it silently so as not to make noise before others. 10. Wherever they are reproved by the prioress, they should immediately seek pardon. 11. Let them not presume to quarrel with anyone, but let them obey their mistress in everything. 12. They are to walk side by side with their companion in processions and not speak in forbidden places or at forbidden times. 13. When any article of clothing is given them, they are to make a profound inclination and say: *Blessed be God in his gifts.* 14. And let them judge no one interiorly. If they see anyone doing something, even if it appears to be evil, let them suppose it to be good or done with a good intention, for human judgment is often mistaken. 15. [Let the mistress instruct them] how they should make the *venia* in chapter or wherever they have been reproved; 16. how they should take the discipline frequently, either by their own hand or someone else's; 17. that they should not speak of the absent unless it is something good. 18. that they must drink with both hands (on the cup) and sitting down; 19. that they ought to care diligently for the books, clothes and other goods of the monastery; 20. how fervent they ought to be in prayer and work.

XIII. HOW NOVICES ARE TO BE RECEIVED

1. When those to be received come to us, let them be led into the chapter at the arrangement of the prioress and some discreet sisters. 2. When they have been led in, they shall prostrate themselves in the middle of the chapter. 3. On being asked by the prioress what they seek, they are to

respond: *God's mercy and yours*. 4. Then they arise at the command of the prioress, who shall expound to them the austerities of the Order and ask them what their will is. 5. If they respond that they are willing to observe everything and to renounce the world, according to the formula: *I, N., vow and promise to God and the blessed Virgin and blessed Mary Magdalene that I will live in religion for the rest of my life and never return to the world, and I sign here in testimony to this thing*; then the prioress says, after other things: *May God who has begun [this good work] in you, bring it to perfection.* And the community responds: *Amen.* 6. Then, once their hair has been cut and disposed of and their secular clothing laid aside, the prioress shall receive them into the sisterhood of the community.

7. No one is to be received unless she is asked whether she is married or a serf, whether she is bound by debts or another religious profession, and whether she has

any hidden infirmity. 8. If she is found to have any (of these impediments), she is not to be received unless for a serious reason of usefulness or danger. 9. It is not our custom to have a year's probation.

XIV. THE MANNER OF PROFESSION

1. This is the formula for profession: *I, N., make profession and promise obedience to God and the blessed Virgin Mary and blessed Mary Magdalene and to you, prioress of this place, according to the rule and customs* [consuetudines] *of your Order, that I will be obedient to you and to your successors until death.*

XV. SILENCE

1. Our sisters shall keep silence in the cloister, the dormitory, the work room, the refectory and the oratory of the sisters. 2. They may speak in other places with

special permission, except that they may speak quietly in the work room, but it must be about the work. 3. The prioress may speak quietly and modestly at table, in such a way as not to interrupt the reader. 4. The sick who are not in bed should keep silence from the main meal until Vespers, as well as after the signal which is given after Compline. At the time of bloodletting, the same silence is observed after the first day on which blood has been let. 5. This is the penalty for breaking silence: For the first offence, the psalm *Have mercy on me God* [Ps. 51] and the *Our Father* are said; likewise for the second offence. For the third offence, the discipline is given; likewise for the fourth, fifth, and sixth offences. For the seventh offence, she shall fast on bread and water while sitting on the ground, and this at the main meal, not at supper. 6. They are not to count past seven offences, but begin the count over again. 7. All this is understood as taking place between two chapters, so that they begin to count breaks of silence from one chapter to the next. 8. They may receive the disciplines privately or with the other sisters after Compline. 9. If another discipline is imposed [for some other reason], when chapter is held, she should receive it there.

10. If anyone has offended her sister in any way, she should cast herself at the other's feet until she is placated and raises her up.

XVI. CLOTHING

1. *Those who are in the houses of kings are clothed in soft garments* (Lk 7, 25). Women who have renounced the world ought to be roughly and humbly clad. 2. For this reason, we propose that the sisters use coarse underclothing. 3. The woolen garments which we use are not to be overly fine or smooth on the outside, but let the rule be carried out: "Let not your habit attract attention, for you should not

strive to please by clothing but by your manner of life."[28] 3. It is sufficient for the sisters to have two tunics with a pelt undergarment.[29] 4. The pelt undergarment is not to be worn except covered by the tunic; similarly, the sheepskin is to be covered by the mantle. The pelt undergarment is to be shorter that the tunic, approximately the length of the scapular, so that it does not show. 5. Neither the sisters nor the friars are to be clothed in pelts or coverings from wild animals. 6. The tunic and the mantle should reach to the ground; the scapular will be one palm-breadth shorter. 7. They are to have shoes and stockings as are necessary and resources permit. They are not to have headscarves.

---

[28] Rule of Augustine, chapter 4

[29] *pellicium*. Probably a lambskin is meant.

XVII. THE TONSURE

Tonsuring and washing of the head are to take place as the rule specifies. [Chap. X]

XVIII. FAULTS

We ordain that everything concerning faults be strictly observed as the rule specifies. [Chaps. XI-XV]

XIX. KEEPING THE SECRETS OF THE CHAPTER, HOUSE OR ORDER

1. We strictly command in virtue of the Holy Spirit and obedience that this be observed: No sister shall dare to make public to outsiders the disagreements of the sisters or friars, or the secrets of the chapter or of the house, by which our Order or house could be disturbed or defamed. If anyone should deliberately act to the contrary, she shall be considered as excom-

municated and schismatic, and a destroyer of our Order and the community of the sisters. Until she has made satisfaction she is to be entirely alienated from communion with anyone and will be subject to the penalty due for a very grave fault.

2. We command with equal severity that no one dare, by word or deed of any sort, to work for division or discord among the sisters or the community or the friars. Whoever has attempted to do this will be subject to the above mentioned penalty.

XX. THE ELECTION OF THE PRIORESS.

For the election of the prioress, everything contained in the rule is to be observed. [Chap. XXIV]

XXI. WORK

1. Since, as it is written: *Idleness teaches many evils* (Sir. 33, 27), our sisters ought to devote themselves most diligently to work. 2. A place designated for this purpose will be assigned to them where, at the appointed hours, all may come together and work in common, according to what is allotted to each one. 3. No one is to withdraw herself because of the grace of praying, or for any other reason, without special permission. 4. We legislate that the time for working throughout the whole year, apart from special days, is to be from the time Prime is said until after Compline, except when the sisters ought to pause for the Divine Office or refectory. However, during the summer, they will be permitted to rest from after dinner until None. 5. At the signal given after Compline all should leave the church for their beds, and both the church and the dormitory, in fact the

whole cloister, should be carefully closed. And let them go to sleep early, so that they may be able to rise for Matins quickly and without drowsiness. 7. If anyone wishes to work after Matins, we do not forbid it.

8. The younger sisters shall learn to read and sing, so that they may be prepared to carry out the Divine Office; it is not wise for them to read books for learning grammar, or other authors. 9. Sisters who have passed the age of twenty-four should not begin to learn the psalter if they do not already know it. 10. Those who have completed twenty years of age and have not already learned music or the chant, should nevertheless learn the psalter, but not bother with the rest.

11. No sister is to dare harass or ask her relatives for gifts, thus remaining in the world by obtaining the things she desires.[30] 12. In the same way, no sister or friar of our

---

[30] The editor observes that this number and the following would fit better in Chapter 26.

Order is to make a contract to act as baptismal or confirmation sponsor for anyone, since it was decreed at the Lateran Council that secular clerics should not do this.[31]

XXII. HOUSES

1. Our sisters should have modest and humble houses, so that they themselves are not burdened with expenses, nor are others, whether seculars or religious, scandalized by the sumptuousness of our buildings.

2. Neither our sisters nor our friars are to be dispensers of the goods or money of others. 3. They may, however, be the depositories. 4. They are not to accept a large number of Masses. 5. Also, they shall not do for themselves anything that may be done with the goods of the house, unless it

---

[31] Literally: "Make a contract of *compaternitatem* or *commaternitatem* with anyone." The editor observes that no evidence of such a decision can be found in any of the Councils of the Lateran.

be for common utility.

XXIII. FEAST DAYS

Our sisters and friars are to observe the solemnities of the saints as the rule prescribes [Chap. XXI, 2], and on those days they shall refrain from manual labor.

XXIV. THE SISTERS SHOULD NOT LEAVE THE ENCLOSURE EXCEPT IN FOUR INSTANCES[32]

1. Our sisters are never to leave their enclosure except in these instances: an invading army, fire, flood or severe famine. 2. Therefore, when it is necessary for someone to go out for any of the aforesaid reasons, they will take companions with

---

[32] The compiler of these statutes joined the legislation current at the time for cloistered nuns (#1) with the provisions from the friars' constitutions regarding their conduct on journeys and preaching missions. The result is unintentionally absurd.

them whom the prioress will appoint as she sees fit for their manner of life and good character. 3. When they have received the blessing, they are to conduct themselves with religious decorum and respectability wherever they go, always avoiding familiarity with suspicious companions. 4. Whenever they are outside the monastery, they are to say their Office as they know and are able, and let them be content with the Office of the churches in which they stay. 5. Whoever is first in rank shall be superior while on the journey, unless perhaps the prioress appointed somebody else before they set out. 6. The companion who has been given to a sister shall obey her in everything as if she were her prioress. 7. With regard to inclinations, sisters on a journey should conform to the customs of the places where they stay. 8. They are to carry testimonial letters with them. 9. Our lay brothers are to do likewise, when they are sent to distant places. 10. The sisters should not accept small gifts from men, nor bestow them; in the same way, the friars should not accept from or give gifts to women.

XXV. RECEIVING LAY BROTHERS AND SISTERS

1. When lay brothers and sisters are received, let them make a vow of continence, renounce property and promise obedience to the prioress in everything. 2. They are not permitted to obligate themselves to the observances of the Order.

3. These are the things they will be bound to observe, insofar as they are able: that in all things they shall serve the community devotedly according to whatever is assigned to them, whether within or outside the house. 4. They shall rise at the same time as the community and make the inclinations in the same way. 5. When they have gotten up for Matins, they are to say the *Our Father* and *Apostles' Creed*, which

they should also do before Prime and after Compline. 6. During Matins, having said the *Our Father* and *Apostles' Creed,* they are to stand up, saying: *Lord, open my lips,* etc., *Glory to the Father.* 7. For Matins on ordinary days, let them say the *Our Father* twenty-four times and at the end: *Glory to the Father; Lord have mercy, Christ have mercy, Lord have mercy, Our Father.* 8. Having said that, they should add: *Through our Lord; Let us bless the Lord,* etc. 9. However, on feasts of nine readings, let them say forty *Our Father's*; at Vespers, fourteen. 10. At all the other hours, let them say seven *Our Father's.* Let them do this in silence, in church or wherever they may be, 12. And they should always conclude with *Through our Lord* and *Let us bless the Lord.* 13. In place of Pretiosa let them say three *Our Father*'s, 14. and for the blessing at meals, one *Our Father* with *Glory be to the Father.*

15. After the meal, for thanks-

giving, let them say three *Our Father's, Glory to the Father,* or *Have mercy on me, God* [Ps. 51], if they know it. 16. As to fasts, food, and abstinence, they should do what the community does. 17. Nevertheless, for the sake of their work, the prioress can dispense them.

18. Both the lay brothers and lay sisters shall have the same amount and kind of clothing as the other sisters, except that it suffices for the brothers' tunics to come down to the ankle, while the scapulars are shorter. 19. The lay brothers are not to wear cappas that are stitched together or closed, but in their place a wide scapular, both sides [i.e., front and back] going down beyond the hands and long enough to reach the shoes, which come up to the calf. 20. The brothers are not to have a mantle. 21. The brothers will not wear leggings,[33]

---

[33] *Occreas*. The word covers everything from soldiers' greaves to peasants' leggings. "Shin guards" might be a good translation.

but they may have woolen mitts.[34] 22. They are to sleep with belted tunic and shoes, and without mattresses, unless by chance they do not have straw or some other such thing upon which to sleep. 23. The scapulars of the lay sisters will not have capuces attached, 24. and their mantles will be gray colored.

25. The lay sisters shall not eat in the refectory with the other sisters nor sleep in their dormitory, but apart in the place assigned to them. 26. Likewise, the brothers will eat apart from the sisters and sleep in their own place. 27. Also, the lay sisters will not tell their faults in chapter together with the other sisters, but the prioress or some other discreet and mature sister can hear their faults apart, for the good of peace and to preserve their devotion.

---

[34] *Manivolas.* Translation conjectural.

28. The lay brothers shall never enter the enclosure, except in those instances that are also permitted to seculars.

29. Neither the lay brothers nor the lay sisters will have a voice in the election of the prioress, the reception of sisters, and similar votes of the chapter, nor is their consent required.

XXVI. SUFFRAGES FOR THE DEAD

1. From the feast of St. Denis until Advent, for the anniversary of all the brothers and sisters, a friar priest shall celebrate three Masses, a sister shall recite the psalter, the lay brothers and sisters shall say fifty *Our Father's.* 2. Let them do the same for a deceased brother or sister of their own convent. Also, for a deceased brother or sister of another convent of our Order, when their death has been announced, each priest should celebrate one Mass and each convent should celebrate one conventual Mass, while each sister or brother should

say the seven penitential psalms or fifty *Our Father's*. 3. The anniversary of fathers and mothers should be kept solemnly on the third day after the feast of Purification with Vigils, Vespers, and the conventual Mass of the day. 4. The anniversary of our benefactors and friends[35] is to be kept in the same way on the third day after the Nativity of Our Lady.

[35] *Familiarum.* Those who attach themselves to the community to serve on a volunteer basis, without legal bonds. Dominicans have always recognized the obligation to pray for friends who help in this way.

APPENDIX

Foundation of the Order of Penitents

According to the narrative of the chronicler of Colmar

The order of women, which is called Penitents, is said to have begun in this way. There was a certain cleric named Rudolph who was serving the Lord faithfully according to his ability. While he was on duty in the area of Worms and was going from village to village ministering to their needs, he found some prostitutes living at a crossroad. When he had reached them, the Spirit of the Lord stirred within him and he wanted to thrash the whores with his walking staff. But they said: "Sir, we are so weak, we can't get food anywhere. Just give us some bread and water and we will do anything you want." When he heard this, he brought them into the city, rented a house for them and shut them up securely in it. There he provided food for them, insofar as he was able. To that end he hired a servant who begged bread for them daily throughout the city. However, people had compassion for them and supplied their necessities in abundance, and in many different ways they commended the deed of the said Rudolph.

Rudolph, seeing that what he had done pleased many, visited various other cities, took prostitutes and supplied their needs in the above mentioned manner. Rudolph himself gave the religious habit to these women and named them, in Latin, *Penitentes*, in German, *Ruwerin.* Their habit consisted in a white tunic, a long white scapular, a long mantle and linen *peplum,* and a white linen veil on the head.

This Rudolph traveled to the pope, had himself made their superior and obtained confirmation of the Order. They could exit from their enclosure for their necessary business and make confession freely to whomever they wished: whether to their chaplains, to common priests, to canons, to black monks or to white,[36] to Friars Minor or Friars Preachers. They principally adhered to these latter for confession and counsel. In fact, they adhered to the Preachers to make greater progress in religion, in riches and in honor.

In the year of the Lord 1288, Lord John Tusculanus, legate to Teutonia, released the master of the Penitents and faithfully commended them to Brother Herman, provincial of the Order of Preachers, that he might direct and govern them.

From: *De rebus Alsaticis ineuntis saeculi XIII - Annales Colmarienses, Basileenses...* M.G.H. SS. XVII, p. 234

---

[36] i.e., Benedictines and Cistercians